Wendy Doniger is the author of several acclaimed and bestselling works, among them, *Winged Stallions and Wicked Mares: Horses in Indian Myth and History*; *The Hindus: An Alternative History*; *The Ring of Truth: Myths of Sex and Jewelry*; *Dreams, Illusion and Other Realities*; and translations of the *Rig Veda* and the *Kamasutra* (with Sudhir Kakar). She is the Mircea Eliade Distinguished Service Professor of the History of Religions at the University of Chicago, Emerita. She has also taught at the School of Oriental and African Studies, University of London, and the University of California, Berkeley.

ALSO BY WENDY DONIGER

The Hindus: An Alternative History

The Ring of Truth: Myths of Sex and Jewelry

Beyond Dharma: Dissent in the Ancient Indian Sciences of Sex and Politics

Reading The Kamasutra: Essays on Vatsyayana's Masterpiece

Winged Stallions and Wicked Mares: Horses in Indian Myth and History

The Dream Narrative

Dreams of God and Mortals in Classical Hinduism

Wendy Doniger

SPEAKING TIGER

TIGERBACKS | Speaking Tiger Short Non-Fiction

SPEAKING TIGER BOOKS LLP
125A, Ground Floor, Shahpur Jat, near Asiad Village,
New Delhi 110049

Published by Speaking Tiger Books in 2021

ISBN: 978-93-5447-215-2
eISBN: 978-93-5447-216-9

10 9 8 7 6 5 4 3 2 1

Typeset in Garamond Premier Pro by SÜRYA, New Delhi
Printed at Chaman Enterprises, New Delhi

CONTENTS

INTRODUCTION

Dreams are a serious matter, indeed seriously material, in classical Hinduism.[1] The Hindu attitude to dreams is part of a more general Hindu attitude to illusion, called *maya*. The entire material world is regarded, theoretically at least, as an illusion wrought by God for His (or Her, or Their) pleasure, for the game, the sport (*lila*). In a very basic sense, the universe (including ourselves) is a dream dreamt by God. This does not necessarily mean that it, and we, are unreal, though certain idealistic forms of Indian religions, both Buddhist and Hindu, do take this tack. On the contrary, for most South Asians it means that our own dreams are, in a sense, synchronized with those of the author of the universe and hence one of the most reliable sources of insight into the reality of that universe.

Dreams and illusions are alike in many ways, but they are also different in many ways, and each teaches us something about reality. Each deals with a form of mental transformation, and with the epistemological problems raised by those transformations. The overarching illusion (*maya*) that the material universe (sometimes referred to as *brahma*, the divine principle that is the ultimate reality) is real at all is seldom visible to us; but we can sense it, sometimes, through the minor illusions or mistaken perceptions (*bhrama*) that Indian philosophers (such as Shankara) discuss at some length: the rope mistaken for a snake, the shell mistaken for silver. Dreams, too, are often retroactively recognized as mistaken perceptions, but ones that catapult the dreamers into new understandings of their waking life. One might say that *bhrama* is the key to *brahma*.

One of the most enchanting and stimulating unsolved riddles is the paradox of the dream within the dream, or the dreamer dreamt. In its broadest outlines, this is a theme that has intrigued philosophers and poets throughout the world. Plato pointed out that it was never possible, at any given moment, to prove 'whether we are asleep and our thoughts are a dream, or whether we are awake and talking with each other in a waking condition.'[2] The idea that we might be characters in someone else's dream—more precisely, in God's dream—recurs in many of the footnotes to Plato, notably in Bishop Berkeley. And in a footnote to Berkeley, Ronald Knox wrote this limerick:

> There once was a man who said, 'God
> Must think it exceedingly odd
> If he finds that this tree
> Continues to be
> When there's no one about in the Quad.'

To which a now unknown poet replied:

> Dear Sir:
> Your astonishment's odd;
> I am always about in the Quad.
> And that's why the tree
> Will continue to be
> Since observed by
> Yours faithfully,
> God

In literature, we encounter this theme of 'God the dreamer' in Calderón's play *Life Is a Dream* and in Lewis Carroll's works (as a satire on Berkeley).[3] The more specific theme of the dream adventure—of the hero who undergoes apparently real experiences for years but awakens to find that only a moment has passed—was elaborately developed in China and Japan and occurs in Islamic and Spanish sources as well. Roger Caillois, who has collected many dream adventures of this type, notes some of its recurrent motifs,

> Someone, in a dream, wakes up—or rather believes that he has awakened, although he continues to dream—and now lies expecting another awakening, which this time may be real but may also be as illusionary as the first. In this way he will be transported from one dream to another, from one awakening to another, without ever being absolutely certain whether he has finally arrived at the true awakening, the one that will restore him to the world of reality...Since, at every moment of the dream, the sleeper is unaware of the fact that he is dreaming, and is even convinced that he is awake, it is clear that

> there can never be a moment in which a person who believes himself to be awake does not have to entertain the suspicion of a doubt that he might perhaps at that time actually be dreaming. This problem has benefited from a long and complex philosophical history.[4]

Closely related to the question of whether we are dreaming or being dreamt is the corollary question of whether we are dramatists or the characters in someone else's dramas. Shakespeare was drawn back to this riddle again and again, in plays dealing with the themes of dreams and illusions (such as *The Tempest*, *A Midsummer Night's Dream*, and *The Winter's Tale*), or employing the device of the play within the play (as in *Hamlet* and *Henry* IV, Part I). More recently, the paradox has been taken up by surrealist artists like René Magritte and M.C. Escher, surrealist playwrights like Pirandello (with his characters in search of an author) and Tom Stoppard (with *Rosencrantz and Guildenstern Are Dead* serving as a play within which we may view Shakespeare's already nested play), and in the stories of Jorge Luis Borges[5] and Mircea Eliade.[6]

When we look at the distribution of this theme more closely, we begin to see a pattern, a complex *mandala* that has India as its center. While Plato was expounding the idealism that we think of as Platonic, Indian sages were composing the even more idealistic Upanishads. The Chinese and Japanese stories were based on tales carried to the Far East by Indian Buddhists; and the Spanish stories were retellings of tales brought by Islamic traders from India. Moreover, whereas the story of the dreamer dreamt was regarded in the West primarily as an exotic delicacy, an appetizer to titillate the mind for a while before one got down to serious philosophizing, in India it was the main course, philosophically speaking; it was taken very seriously indeed, as an elusive clue to a real truth. As Caillois remarks of the dream adventure in European romantic literature,

> Very frequently the dream remains a fairy tale that is dispelled by the awakening and to which at times a cumbersome allegorical value is attributed; it has nothing in common with the intellectual complications

> of the Oriental dream. 'It was only a dream,' the sleeper cries out upon awakening, occasionally disappointed, occasionally relieved, all according to whether the dream gratified or oppressed him. It is never more than an illusion, which may have been pleasing or distressing, but which the opening of the eyelids suffices to send back into nothingness.[7]

In India, by contrast, the dream adventure often proves the very opposite point, the 'nothingness' of the world that we see when we open our eyes, or the substantial reality of the dream itself.

THE DOCTRINE OF ILLUSION IN THE YOGAVASISHTHA

The most complex example of the dream within a dream narrative that I know occurs in a Sanskrit text called the *Yogavasishtha-maharamayana*, composed in Kashmir probably sometime between the tenth and twelfth century of our era.[8] This text is well loved by Indians; it has been translated into many of the vernacular Indian languages and has found its way into 'anonymous' oral traditions.[9] It is a curious blend of abstract, classical Indian philosophy and vivid, detailed Indian folklore, a kind of *Reader's Digest* or *Classic Comic* version of the doctrine of illusion. In it, a philosophy that often seems hollowly inhuman comes to life when the narrative spells out its wildest implications. It is as if someone took the abstract concept, 'The universe is unreal', and made it somehow anthropomorphic, producing a kind of teaching device to make us understand what it *feels* like to realize that everything is unreal. And, of course, it can't be done; in our hearts, we don't believe it. But the narrative allows us—nay, forces us—to imagine ourselves in a situation in which we *must* believe it, in which we must act out the paradox.

The story in the *Yogavasishtha* is about two philosophical ideas: it is about the way the mind apprehends the world, and about the way the world is. More particularly, it is about the way the two problems are related, the way our minds affect the world, and the way the world exists in our minds. It is a kind of religious parable, but more than that, it is a metaparable, a parable about parables, for it is *about* storytelling, as well as an example of storytelling. It builds the philosophy into the story by placing a running commentary in the mouths of several of the central characters, and it builds our minds—the minds of us, the audience, as we listen to the tale—into the text by drawing us deeper and deeper into the tale within the tale. In this way it embodies and talks about the paradox of the author who is a character in someone else's story, the dreamer who is a figure in someone else's dream.

The Monk Who Met The People in His Dreams

Once upon a time there was a monk who was inclined to imagine things rather a lot. He would meditate and study all the time, and fast for days on end. One day this fancy came to him: 'Just for fun, I will experience what happens to ordinary people.' As soon as he had this idea, his thought somehow took the form of another man, and that man wished for an identity and a name, even though he was just made of thought. And by pure accident, as when a crow happens to be under a tree when a palm fruit falls from it and hits him, he thought, 'I am Jivata.'

This dream man, Jivata, enjoyed himself for a long time in a town made in a dream. There he drank too much and fell into a heavy sleep, and in his dream he saw a Brahmin who read all day long. One day that Brahmin fell asleep, worn out from the day's work, but those daily activities were still alive within him, like a tree inside a seed, and so he saw himself, in a dream, as a prince. One day that prince fell asleep after a heavy meal, and in his dream he saw himself as a king who ruled many lands and indulged in every sort of luxury. One day that king fell asleep, having gorged himself on his every desire, and in his dream he saw himself as a celestial woman. That woman fell into a deep sleep in the languor that followed making love, and she saw herself as a doe with darting eyes. That doe one day fell asleep and dreamed that she was a clinging vine, because she had been accustomed to eating vines; for animals dream too, and they always remember what they have seen and heard.

The vine saw herself as a bee, that used to buzz among the vines; the bee fell in love with a lotus in a lotus pond and became so intoxicated by the lotus sap he drank, that his wits became numb one day; and just then an elephant came to that pond and trampled the lotus, and the bee—still attached to the lotus—was crushed with it on the elephant's tusk. As the bee looked at the elephant, he saw himself as an elephant in rut. That elephant in rut fell into a deep pit and became the favorite elephant of a king. One day, the elephant was cut to pieces by a sword in battle and, as he went to his final resting place, he saw a swarm of bees hovering over the sweet ichor that oozed from his temples, and so the elephant became a bee again. The bee returned to the lotus pond and was trampled under the foot of an elephant, and just then he noticed a goose beside him in the pond, and so he became a goose. The goose moved through other births, other wombs, for a long time, until one day, when he was a goose in a flock of other geese, he realized that, being a goose, he was the same as the swan of Brahma, the Creator. Just as he had this thought, he was shot by a hunter and he died, and then he was born as the swan of Brahma.

One day the swan saw the god Rudra, and he thought, with sudden certainty, 'I am Rudra.' Immediately that idea was reflected, like an image in a mirror, and he took on the form of Rudra. This Rudra indulged in every pleasure that entered his mind, living in the palace of Rudra and attended by Rudra's servants. But the Rudra that he had become had a special power of knowledge, and in his mind he could see every single one of his former experiences. He was amazed by the hundred dreams he had had, and he said to himself, 'How wonderful! This complicated illusion fools everyone; what is unreal seems to be real, like water in a desert that turns out to be a mirage. I am something that can be thought, and I have been thought.

'There happened to be a soul that, by chance, became a monk in some universe, and he experienced what he had been thinking about: he became Jivata. But because Jivata admired Brahmins, he saw himself as a Brahmin; and since the Brahmin had thought about princes all the time, he became a prince. And since that prince was inclined to do things in order to run a kingdom, he became a king; and because the king was full of lust, he became a celestial woman. And that fickle woman was so jealous of the beautiful eyes of a doe that she became a doe; and the doe became a vine that she had noticed, and the vine saw herself as a bee that she had observed for a long time, and the bee was trampled under the feet of an elephant that he had seen, and he wandered in and out of a series of rebirths. At the end of the round of a hundred rebirths is Rudra, and I am Rudra, I am he, the one who stands in the flux of rebirths where everyone is fooled by his own mind. For my amusement, I will raise up all those creatures who are my own rebirths, and I will look at them, and by giving them the ability to look at the matter as it really is, I will make them unite into one.'

When Rudra had decided upon this, he went to that universe where the monk was sleeping in his monastery like a corpse. Joining his mind to the monk's mind, Rudra woke him up; and then the monk realized the error he had made (in believing his life as Jivata to be real). And when the monk looked at Rudra, who was the monk himself and was also made of Jivata and the others, he was amazed, though one who was truly enlightened would not have found cause for amazement. Then Rudra and the monk went, the two of them together, to a certain place in a corner of the space of the mind where Jivata had been reborn, and then they saw him asleep, unconscious, still holding a sword in his hand: the corpse of Jivata. Joining their minds to his mind, they woke him up, and then, though they were one, they had three forms: Rudra and Jivata and the monk. Though they were awake, they did not seem to be awake; they were amazed, and yet not amazed, and they stood there in silence for a moment, like images painted in a picture.

Then all three of them went through the sky to the place, echoing in the empty air, where the Brahmin had been reborn, and there they saw the Brahmin in his house, asleep, with his wife—the Brahmin lady—clasping him around his neck. They joined their minds to his mind and woke him up, and they all stood there, overcome with amazement. Then they went to the place where the king had been reborn, and they awakened him with their mind, and then they wandered through the other rebirths until they reached the swan of Brahma. And at that moment they all united together and became Rudra, a hundred Rudras in one.

Then they were all awakened by Rudra and they all rejoiced and looked upon one another's rebirths, seeing illusion for what it was. Then Rudra said, 'Now go back to your own places and enjoy yourselves there with your families for awhile, and then come back to me. And at doomsday, all of us, the bands of creatures who are part of me, will go to the ultimate resting place.' And Rudra vanished, and Jivata and the Brahmin and the others all went back to their own places with their own families, but after a while they will wear out their bodies and will unite

> again back in the world of Rudra, and they will be seen as stars in the sky.[10]

This story is a highly sophisticated variant of a much-loved Indo-European folk motif, which includes the story of Chicken-Licken (who told Henny-Penny who told Foxy-Loxy...that the sky was falling) and The House That Jack Built. The theme also appears in European literature as the motif of 'Magic: Man magically made to believe himself bishop, archbishop, and pope.'[11] But instead of piling up barnyard animals or clergymen, the Indian text piles up nested figments of the imagination.

This extraordinary story speaks directly to us now, even though it is part of a text that was composed in India more than a thousand years ago. It is, I think, possible for us to ask our own questions of this text, but before we can do this, we must first try to understand, as well as we can, what questions the author meant us to ask of it. This task is greatly facilitated for us by the fact that many of these questions are written right into the text. The story of the monk's dream is narrated by the great sage Vasishtha to Prince Rama (the same Rama who is the hero of the great Indian epic *Ramayana*). Rama asks Vasishtha a number of questions, many of them the very questions that would occur to people in our time on first encountering this story—literal-minded, earthbound, rather flat-footed questions, it would seem:

> Rama asked, 'How did Jivata and the Brahmin and the other forms that the monk imagined become real? How can an object of the imagination be real?' Vasishtha said, 'The reality of the imagination is only partial; do not take it for something entirely real. What isn't there, isn't there. Yet the true nature of what is seen in a dream or visualized by the imagination exists at all times. Everything exists in a corner of the mind...A person sees a dream as if it were a hard thing, and then from that dream he falls back into another dream, and from that into yet another dream, and each time it appears hard and firm.' Then Rama asked, 'What became of the hundred Rudras? *Were* they all Rudras, or weren't they? And how could a hundred minds be made from a single mind? How could they be made by that Rudra who was himself made in someone's dream?' Vasishtha replied, 'The monk visualized a

> hundred bodies in a hundred dreams. But all those forms in the dream *were*, in fact, Rudra, a hundredfold Rudra. For those who have removed the veil from reality can imagine things so precisely that those mental perceptions are actually experienced. And because of the omnipresence of the universal soul, something that is experienced in a particular way and in a particular place by a mind with true understanding will actually come into existence in that way at that very place.' [12]

On the one hand, the text seems to say, all the things that we think are real are only parts of a dream—our dream, or someone's else's dream. On the other hand, there *is* a reality in dreams, for the things that we imagine or dream are reflections of some reality that does exist at all times and in all places, and happens to get into *our* minds 'by accident', like the accident that makes the monk think that he is Jivata. In this view, mental images are reflections of an underlying reality; there *was* a Jivata, and the monk dreamt of him; it only remained then for Rudra to find the Jivata that the monk had dreamt of and introduce the two of them. Though the monk dreamed of a hundred people, those people did exist as a part of the god Rudra. Yet the text also implies that the monk had the power to dream them into existence from his mind upward, all the way up the line from the monk to the swan to Rudra; and Rudra had the power to think them all into existence as part of himself, from his mind downward, all the way from the swan to the monk. The text tells us that all the people in the dream are part of Rudra, physically; and it also says that they are part of his mind, his dream. These are not contradictions. For Rudra, to think of something is for him to both make it exist and find that it has always existed. These two kinds of creation—'making' and 'finding'—are the same, for in both cases, the mind imposes its idea upon the spirit/matter dough of reality, cutting it up like a cookie cutter, now into stars, now into hearts, now into elephants, now into swans. It makes them, and it finds them already there, like a sculptor (or a *bricoleur)* making new forms out of *objets trouvés.*[13]

Rudra's mind is the mould that stamps out images, all of which ultimately derive from him. He stamps this mould upon the spirit/matter continuum of the universe in such a way that it breaks up into the separate (or rather, apparently separate) consciousnesses of all of us. The images that he sketches in our minds were already there—in the continuum, and in our minds—but we cannot know them until his mind touches ours, until he 'joins his mind to (our) mind'. Finally, when we *really* know Rudra, the images vanish, and the continuum is seen as it really is—devoid of the fragments of individual figures. Then the background becomes the foreground.

This philosophy is made explicit at many points throughout the text, often in the form of explanatory remarks made by the storyteller (Vasishtha) to clarify what he regards as difficult or important points in the narrative, or in response to questions. It is a philosophy well known in India from the time of the Upanishads, a millennium and a half before our text was composed. Yet it may not have been the predominant cultural assumption, the shared 'common sense', in India at that time.[14] This is, I think, evident from the text's repeated insistence that all the characters in the story were 'amazed' to find that the lives they had taken for real were merely parts of someone else's dreams or that, contrariwise, people they had just dreamed about turned out to be real people they could talk to. They are 'amazed' at *both* implications: that their real lives are dreams and that their dreams are real—or rather, as real as their waking lives. They had assumed, as we usually do, that dreams are unreal and that lives are real. Even at the very end of the story, Rama cannot understand how the hundred Rudras could become real, and the commentator explains his quandary:

> Rama asked his question because he did not think it was possible that the matter could be as it seemed, and as it had just been said to be, as in the verse that stated, 'He awakened the monk, joining mind to mind'—that is, he did not think that one *could* awaken the monk and the others by transferring consciousness from Rudra's mind, or that in that way Rudra could make a hundred people by making the monk have a hundred dreams.[15]

Even Rudra himself is said to have been 'amazed' by his realization that his hundred dreams had thought themselves to be real, though he then conquers his amazement and carefully puzzles it all out.[16]

It must be granted that the narrator's insistence on the 'amazement' of the characters in the story is, in part, a literary device (one that is well known from Christian miracle tales) to emphasize the importance of the extraordinary event and to provide us with doubting fools—fall guys set up either to be converted or to provide a foil for those who are converted. Nevertheless, these 'amazed' participants and bystanders must also represent the point of view that the narrator would have expected to find in at least some of his audience. One might argue that the experience of surprise at reality-switching is more common—and hence less surprising—in India than in the West, since Indian epistemological assumptions make it possible to cross such borders more easily and more often. Yet such a boundary is taken for granted, even in India.[17] The fact that people in cultures outside of India also experience 'amazement' (or even disbelief) when they first hear this story is not, I think, irrelevant. In any case, we will read ourselves into any text that we read; not only *may* we ask our own questions of the text; we cannot *help* asking our own questions. But I would argue that it must have been extremely difficult, if not impossible, for anyone, anywhere, ever to have maintained the extreme form of the belief that the entire universe, including oneself, was totally unreal. Nor does this text, finally, ask its readers to believe this.

The text presents us with a rather extreme philosophical doctrine—that there is no crucial difference, or perhaps, no recognizable or testable difference, between waking reality and dream images. Thus it states that 'truly enlightened people' would *not* have been 'amazed' by the monk's experience. Then it gives us a number of people who *are* astonished when presented with evidence that this might be true. But the paradox does not rest there. Rama asks another set of questions that moves the dilemma onto another level altogether.

When Vasishtha had finished speaking, Rama asked, 'Is there such a monk? Search within yourself and tell me right away.' Vasishtha said, 'Tonight I will go into a deep trance and search the universe to find out if there is such a monk or not, and tomorrow morning I will tell you.' When they met again the next morning, Vasishtha said, 'Rama, I searched for that monk for a long time yesterday, with the eye of knowledge, the eye of meditation. Hoping to see such a monk, I wandered through the seven continents, and over the mountains of the earth, but no matter how far I went, I could not find such a monk; for how could something from the realm of the mind be found outside it? But then, near dawn, once more I went north in my mind, to a glorious country named Jina, where there is a famous monastery built over an anthill. And in that monastery, in the corner of a hut, there was a monk named Far-sight (Dirghadrisha), who had been meditating for twenty-one nights. His own servants did not enter his firmly bolted house, for they feared they might disturb his meditation. In a former eon there was once another monk of this very sort, just as I described him, and this one today is a second. Then, just in play, I searched through other universes, and finally I found, in a universe in the corner of space in the future, another monk just like that, with the same powers. And even in this very assembly there are people who will someday have the very same experiences and take on such a form and do such things, when this illusion will cast its spell over them.'

Then Rama's father, Dasharatha, said to Vasishtha, 'Greatest of sages, let me send my men to the hut of that monk to awaken him and bring him right back here.' Vasishtha said, 'Great King, the body of that monk no longer has the breath of life in it; it is dissolved with rot; it is no longer the vessel of a living creature. The soul of that monk has become the swan of Brahma; during his own lifetime he has been released from life and is no longer subject to rebirth. At the end of a month the monk's servants, longing to see him, will force open the bolts, and they will wash his body and throw it out. Since the monk himself has left that body and has gone somewhere else, how could anyone wake up that ruined corpse in the monastery?'[18]

What are we to make of this epilogue? Rama's question begins to consider the possible reality, not of the characters in the monk's dream, but of the monk himself—that is, the reality status of a character in a story told by Vasishtha. And in his response to Rama, Vasishtha jumps out of the frame of narration and into his own story, just as the monk jumps out of the frame of his dream to meet the people he dreams of—or perhaps, as Rudra jumps out of the frame of his divine mind to meet the thoughts in it. This adds a new dimension to the nested levels of the dream—for now we have Vasishtha 'thinking' of Rudra who is 'realizing' the monk who is 'dreaming' of Jivata and the others. It also adds another figure, Vasishtha, to the list of those who are privileged to manipulate the strings of the puppets within the cosmic drama by giving physical form to their mental images.

Vasishtha is at first sceptical of any possibility that his own mental constructs could be real; as he says to Rama, 'No matter how far I went, I could not find such a monk; for how could something from the realm of the mind be found outside it?'[19] It would appear that, at this point at least, Vasishtha aligns himself with those who are 'amazed' to find their mental creations coming to life. Yet he *does* go to look for the monk, nevertheless. By seeking the monk, Vasishtha acts out the idealistic assumptions of the text, assumptions that have already been challenged by the scepticism of Rama, whose doubts are at first echoed by Vasishtha himself. But Vasishtha finds the monk. By finding him, Vasishtha both discredits that scepticism and greatly strengthens and enhances the idealistic argument, for he demonstrates that not only dreams, but even works of artistic creation—the stories that we make up to prove a point—reflect some aspect of reality, one that most of us do not have the powers to prove as Vasishtha did. This is an important extension, for it implies that this reality is reflected not only in dreams—which we take to be real while dreaming, but which we retroactively define as unreal when we awaken—but even in stories that we take to be unreal from the very start. From the god's-eye view, all stories are true.

Why did Vasishtha think he could find the monk, since the monk was merely a creature in a story he had told and, supposedly, made up himself? The commentary suggests that Rama might have wrestled with this problem before framing his question to Vasishtha:

> Rama was full of doubt and curiosity. He praised his guru and recognized the purpose of his instruction, but he said, 'Search within yourself and ask yourself this question: "Even though I imagined this monk and spoke about him in order to enlighten you, Rama, nevertheless did he actually come into existence somewhere?" For it is simply not possible that a person that you would talk about would not have some sort of true essence.'[20]

Rama was astounded by the tale of the monk's dream; that is, he shared to some extent our 'common sense' intuition that dreams are not real. Yet Rama's question, and Vasishtha's implicit affirmative answer—for he does go to look for the monk—suggest that both of them were at least half-convinced of the real existence of the monk; that is, they shared to some extent the philosophy set forth in the text, in flagrant violation of their common sense. Their ambivalence is explicitly stated: 'they were amazed, and not amazed.' They wanted to find out *for sure*, and so Vasishtha set out to test his hypothesis. Both Rama and Vasishtha felt that there was, in fact, a possibility that Vasishtha's mental creations *might* have a physical reality. This is the psychology of the text. The fact that it never occurred to Vasishtha to go and look for the monk until Rama asked him to do so, and the brusqueness of his initial reply to Rama—'How could you expect to find…'—probably indicate Vasishtha's belief that it does not really matter at all if one finds the specific, 'real' monk of the dream; Vasishtha's didactic point lies elsewhere. Nevertheless, to please Rama, he does go and look, and he is not at all 'amazed' in the end to find that the monk does exist.

The monk's existence might be explained in at least two ways, corresponding to Rudra's 'finding' or 'making' the figures in his dream. Each of these explanations carries with it a different implication about the nature of reality; together they provide an expression of the ontology of the text. The first, implicit in the commentator's gloss, is the possibility that certain people might have the power instinctively to 'tune in' on some real, already existing physical phenomenon—a person, a life, a city—while apparently just imagining such a phenomenon in a spirit of pure play, or by pure chance. This is what Rama means when he says, 'Whatever a person *like you* (i.e., the great sage Vasishtha) would talk about' must have some sort of true essence: such a sage would instinctively make up something *real*, even when constructing a hypothetical case. Later, when Rama asks Vasishtha if the hundred Rudras were real, Vasishtha replies, 'The hundred bodies that the monk saw in his dreams—all of that was just thought up for the sake of explanation, and so I did not talk about them (in detail).'[21] Though Vasishtha did not bother to invent all the details, the details *were there*; Vasishtha just told Rama there were a hundred Rudras, to make his pedagogic point. In the same way, the monk dreamed of Jivata and there *was* a Jivata, whom he later found with Rudra's help. The second explanation is one that the text has already dwelt upon at some length: certain people—of whom Vasishtha is apparently one—have the power to make their mental projections, their dreams, become real physical objects—objects that had not existed until the powerful dreamer dreamed them into reality. In the context of our story, these two explanations are mutually supportive, not contradictory.

Thus when Dasharatha, the king, asks Vasishtha to bring the monk to court, Vasishtha gently points out the stupidity of the question, not on the basis of the argument that one could hardly expect to find the monk at all (the tentative and quickly disproved hypothesis with which Vasishtha had at first ridiculed Rama's question about the reality of the monk), but rather because the monk's body was so *very* real that it had, like all real bodies, eventually ceased to exist; that is, it had rotted away. The reality of that body is brought home to us by the great detail in which the situation at the monk's hut is described, his name, the barred door, the worried servants. (The commentary suggests that Vasishtha said to the king, 'The monk had commanded his servants not to open the bolts of the house for a month, and even your ministers cannot awaken him.'[22]) If, then, the monk is real, either as a result of Vasishtha's creation of him or as the result of some former creation that Vasishtha instinctively recognized when he made up his story, how long has he been real? To put the question more broadly: Do the people in the monk's dream exist for just the one episode that Vasishtha tells us about, perhaps a few months of an adult life, and suddenly vanish when he wakes up or dies, or do they live entire lives, from birth to death, of which the monk witnesses only a brief fragment?

Before we can answer this, we must try to decide whether this is a story about dreams or a story about rebirth. Certainly it is, at least in part, a story about rebirth. When we reach the point where Rudra begins to retrace his footsteps, as it were, he refers to the 'flux of rebirth (*samsara*) in which one is deluded by one's own mind' and the 'various wildernesses of rebirth' through which he has wandered.[23] Rudra then goes from one universe to another to find the place where the rebirth (never the birth) of Jivata, the Brahmin, and so forth had taken place, or of even greater significance, had *begun*. And at the end, they all wander together in the grounds of other rebirths. For *samsara* primarily denotes the physical world in which creatures circulate through their repeated births and deaths.

The figures at the beginning and the end of the chain of the monk's dream, directly inside the outer frame formed by the monk and Rudra, are a man named Jivata and a swan. Jivata (the only character in the dream who is given a proper name) is a derivative of *jiva*, the ordinary Sanskrit word used to denote the individual life or the transmigrating soul. The swan is an ancient Indian symbol for the soul, and more specifically, for the returning soul, the transmigrating soul, based perhaps on the natural symbolism of the swan's migration. More particularly, the swan may symbolize the memory of past lives, as in a verse from a Sanskrit poem describing the moment when a princess came of age: 'When the time came for her to learn, all the knowledge from her former life came back to her, as the rows of swans come back to the Ganges in the autumn.'[24] In another variant of the story of the dream of rebirth, a king who is reborn as a woman meets a friend from his previous life as a king, who tells him, 'Don't you remember your old friend? You and I, my dear, were two swans who lived together in the lake of the mind, until you left me to wander on earth. I created the illusion that made you think you were a man or a woman. Our true nature is as two swans.' And when the swan of the mind was awakened by the other swan, he won back the memory that he had lost.[25] In this text, the swans are explicitly identified with the individual soul and the universal soul, and explicitly said to be one and the same.

In this sense, each of the levels within the monks' dream is a complete rebirth of a single soul that goes from Rudra to the monk to Jivata to the Brahmin and so forth, until it subsides back into Rudra again. This mechanism is clearly at work in the second half of the cycle, when the animals die and are reborn, presumably as young animals that grow up. On the other hand, it appears that the monk transfers his consciousness into an already existent Jivata, taking up Jivata's life *in medias res*, as it were, and Jivata joins consciousness with an already existent middle-aged Brahmin, and so forth. This mechanism would explain how all of them continued to exist when the monk awoke, and how they were able to meet and talk together when Rudra found them all. Once again, the text says both that the soul 'makes' each new life (from birth to death) and that it 'finds' its new lives (in midstream). There is one single soul, and there are a hundred different souls, and yet they are the same.

We do not see the entire rebirth of each of the characters; none of them is born, and most do not die within the story. The monk falls into a deep trance; Jivata passes out in a drunken stupor; the Brahmin falls asleep after a hard days' reading; the king and the celestial harlot are exhausted by pleasure; and so forth. These people dream and become what they have *habitually* dreamt about. Yet, near the end of the chain, some of the animals do seem to die and become what they happen to see at the moment of death: the bee is pulverized on the tusk of an elephant; the elephant is cut to pieces by a sword; the bee is trampled by another elephant. The elephant is actually (if euphemistically) said to have died, and the others experience violent accidents. The penultimate transition is explicitly said to be a death: the goose dies, shot by a hunter, and becomes the swan of Brahma. The swan then experiences the final and most subtle transition: as soon as he realizes that he is Rudra, his idea is instantly reflected like an image in a mirror—that is, it is projected outside of himself and takes the form of a solid figure, or if you prefer, it is reflected in the already existing figure of Rudra himself. The swan then takes the form of Rudra and abandons his (swan) body, just as the scent of a cluster of blossoms leaves the blossoms behind and wafts away on the wind.[26]

It would appear that the figures are arranged in a kind of hierarchy, and that the higher consciousnesses merely dream of a partial rebirth, while the lower ones must actually die, must endure physically what the others have merely experienced mentally. Setting aside for the moment the monk, as a special case to which we will return, we can see that the characters form three groups that steadily descend in metaphysical acuity. Jivata is defined as an ordinary sort of man who loves life; hence he is the logical starting point for an odyssey that is designed to dramatize the doctrines of illusion and rebirth for ordinary people—the ones who are 'amazed' when the dividing line between dream and reality melts away. He is, moreover, the random sample, the man in the street; the monk thinks of him 'by pure chance'.[27] Jivata is the literal embodiment of the transmigrating soul—of Everyman. Paired with Jivata, we encounter the highest human type: the learned Brahmin. The monk, the outermost dreamer, actively sets out to produce the dream experience and to materialize it; and this activity, as we shall see, is proper only to perfected monks, not to ordinary Brahmins. Thus, the Brahmin and Jivata are rightly paired as puppets, rather than puppeteers, in this particular episode. There is, of course, one other Brahmin in the story—Vasishtha—but his role is even more peculiar than that of the monk, and we must postpone for the moment an analysis of his status in the hierarchy.

After the Brahmin come the prince and the king. The royal image is divided into two, of which the first is lower than the second, as was the case with our first pair.

Below the king is a triad of females who form the transition from higher to lower consciousness, one semidivine (the celestial woman), one animal (the doe), and one vegetable (the vine). These three figures are still part of the higher echelon who dream rather than die, and who become what they have always known, not what they see as they die. The text tells us that animals do dream. So, too, is the vine conscious; she is said to see in herself the embodiment of the loveliness that had been asleep and numb inside the doe for a long time.[28] The vine is the incarnation of the metaphor of female beauty—graceful women are always like clinging vines in Sanskrit poetry—even as Jivata is the embodiment of the soul.

The next quartet, like the first, is divided into two pairs. The elephant and the bee are animals closely associated with violence and eroticism. The wildness of the male elephant in rut carries fairly obvious symbolic meaning, and bees in Indian love poetry are said to form the bowstring of the god of lust, and to plunge deep inside the flowers that ooze with sap even as the elephant's temples ooze with ichor. In our text, the bee perishes because his lust for the lotus stupefies him and makes him stick to her even in death.[29] The bee and the elephant find violent deaths, over and over again.

Then we encounter the last pair, the goose who becomes a swan. Here the hierarchy doubles back on itself; the lowest becomes the highest, and the swan becomes the god Rudra. The true break comes within this pair: the goose has to be shot dead to become the swan, the only explicit death in the story and the most violent transition. Whereas the swan merely 'reflects' itself into Rudra, the least violent transition. Once we have reached the swan, we are home. At this point, there is no more dreaming; now we begin to unravel all that has been dreamt.

The creatures in the monk's dream form a pattern that is a masterful combination of order and chance. They are distributed to cover the full spectrum of consciousness, a point that the text emphasizes by its overall groupings: human males, nonhuman females, and male animals and insects. These groups are, I think, meant to depict a steady general decline. Yet within each group there are upswings—Jivata moves up when he becomes a Brahmin or a prince; the bee improves his lot when he becomes an elephant; and the goose becomes a very special swan. Moreover, there are switchbacks (the elephant who relapses into bee-hood), redundancies (several bees), and finally a catchall group of 'etceteras' at the end. These irregularities convey the richness and randomness of the process of reincarnation.

This random variation also characterizes the pattern through which all of us will, at some time before the end of infinity, become incarnate as that same monk, in much the same way as the monkey playing at his typewriter will eventually compose the complete works of Shakespeare. Yet, although anything *can* happen, certain things are more *likely* to happen; this is the way that karma skews and orders the chaos of the universe. As the same dream gets into different peoples' heads—in this case, the dream of the monk who meets the people in his dreams—there may be minor variations on the theme, minor changes in the manifestations of the archetype: 'Again and again these lives revolve in creation, like the waves in water, and some (rebirths) are strikingly similar (to what they were before), and others are about half the same; some are a little bit the same, some are not very much alike at all, and sometimes they are once again just the same.'[30] This flexibility, together with the elements of pure chance and the gravity of karmic tendencies, makes certain coincidences not only possible, but probable.

Midway through the round of rebirths, the text moves from dreams to deaths, and then begins to talk of them simultaneously, using the two images to illuminate one another: death is like a dream (or, rather, like an awakening), and a dream or an illusion is experienced as a kind of death. We 'awaken' from ignorance, or from sleep, or from life; the same verb covers all three. Ultimately, the contrast between creatures who dream and creatures who die is exposed as being as meaningless as the contrast between one transmigrating soul and a hundred dreamt souls. Illusion and rebirth melt together from the very start in the short poem (in the commentary) that introduces the whole story: 'The story of Jivata is about the way in which people wrongly perceive that they have obtained various bodies; such a wrong perception operated in the mind of the monk as a result of his various karmic memory traces (*vasanas*).'[31]

For this is not just a story about rebirth, it is a story about karma. What are these karmic memory traces? In classical Indian philosophy, on which our text constantly draws, they are the bits of experience that adhere to the transmigrating soul and that predispose it to act in one way or another in its new life. They may also be experienced as inexplicable, tantalizing memories, the uneasy aftermath of a dream that has been forgotten by the conscious mind but that continues to haunt the deeper mind—the subconscious or unconscious mind, as the Freudians and Jungians would term it. It was the karmic memory traces that kept alive the knowledge that returned to the princess when she came of age, like swans returning to the Ganges in autumn. Our text tells us, for example, that after the bee had become an elephant and was then reborn as a bee, he went back to the same lotus pond where he had previously met with his unfortunate accident, 'because people who are not aware of their karmic traces find it hard to give up their bad habits.'[32] So too, when the beautiful woman becomes a doe, because she envies the beauty of the doe's eyes, Rudra remarks, 'Alas, the delusion that results from the karmic traces causes such misery among creatures.'[33] All of the people in the dream-chain are reborn in a particular form because *they want something.* There is a hunger left unsated in their present lives, and this propels them across the barrier of death into a new birth, where that still unfulfilled longing leads them to do what they do. The link between dream illusions and the compulsions that make us fall again and again into the trap of rebirth is carefully forged by our text:

> One's own soul, making separate what is in
> fact a unity, becomes fragmented in rebirths;

> every single creature dies and experiences, as a separate existence, a life that is like a dream. It is not only the monk whose soul quickens from a previous life; our own living souls go from one delusion to another delusion, every day. Just as a cloud, that seems hard as a rock, is shattered on the tip of a mountain, so the living soul is shattered upon the Supreme Soul.[34]

The one thing that is real—firm and hard—is the universal soul, the Godhead. The experience of the individual soul, by contrast, is entirely soft, a cloud of karmic traces. The individual soul is a dream, but there *is* something firm in the universe, something real—the universal soul of which each living soul is a fragment.

The monk is the one who understands this. He is free from the unfulfilled longings that animate the creatures of his dreams. The monk, at the top of the human hierarchy, is the point at which the dream and the rebirth converge and diverge. Rudra says that the monk was a soul that by chance became a monk; when Rudra returns to find the monk and awaken him (in the main story, before the epilogue), the monk is asleep *as if* he were a corpse; he is the dreaming soul. In the epilogue, however, when Vasishtha goes inside the story himself to find the monk, he finds only a dead body: the soul has escaped and gone back to Rudra, and the monk *is* nothing but a corpse. Thus the monk is the soul that *seems* to be born and die, though the soul is, in fact, merely dreaming, and being dreamt. The monk's story acts out the basic metaphor of the text: that what seems to be life and death is merely a dream and an awakening.

The monk's involvement in rebirth is different from that of all the other characters in Vasishtha's story (or within the monk's dream). The text insists that the monk himself was born purely 'by chance', and that he in turn became Jivata 'by accident'.[35] That is, the monk did *not* become reborn to quench a thirst, but merely dreamed of another life out of pure intellectual curiosity. He becomes Jivata merely 'in play', or 'for amusement' (*lilartham*),[36] the word for purposeless sport being the same as the one used in classical philosophical texts to describe why it is that God, who has no desires, bothers to make the universe at all. Rudra repeats that the monk indulged in pure play when he imagined Jivata,[37] and it is this same spirit of pure play that leads Rudra himself to decide to travel through the universes to wake up all the figures in the monk's dream.[38]

This is what sets the monk apart from all the others: he alone can control his mental imaging, which means both that he is not forced, willy-nilly, to become what he does not want to be (or for that matter, what he wants to be), and also that he can project his own mental images onto other minds or onto the fabric of reality itself. The text takes pains to tell us about this: it was the purity of his mind, and the powers developed in meditation, that gave him the ability to become whatever he thought of; that is, he emptied his mind of all but the one thing he wanted to become, so that he *was* nothing but that thought. The commentator is even more specific about the monk's powers: in the manner of ascetics (*yatis*), he assumed the form of another man,[39] for yogis can enter other peoples' real, existing bodies. This is a common motif in Indian folk tales.

Yet the monk is caught up, like the others, in his own imaginings; like them, he is astonished when brought face to face with the people in his dreams, and Rudra says that the monk became Jivata because of his still decaying karmic memory traces.[40] He experiences precisely what they all experience, even though, unlike them, he sets out to do it on purpose. Thus the introductory verse tells us that the monk was the victim of a mistaken perception (*vibhrama*),[41] for he took the people in his dream to be real and he did not, on the other hand, realize at first that he was merely part of Rudra's dream. As soon as he wished to become someone else, his mind lost its calm, like an ocean stirred by a whirlpool.[42] When Rudra replays the story in his own mind, he says that the monk's form changed because of the emotion that moved him at the time.[43] Rama is puzzled by this problem and asks Vasishtha how a monk of such spiritual distinction could be caught up in the web of delusion.[44] Vasishtha does not answer this question specifically, but the subsequent analysis makes it clear that the monk's great degree of mental control, though temporarily swept aside by the intensity of the dream, reasserted itself, so that the monk could realize the dream of Rudra, and could become awakened. Thus the commentator introduces the last chapter with this verse: 'In this chapter, the body of the monk is destroyed when he has been released through his meditation, and just as the monk was first bound by and then released from his false perception, so, too, other people become bound and are released at their own awakenings.'[45] The monk is part of the chain gang of rebirth, like all the rest of us, but he is first in line, and this text describes the moment when he breaks out, to set an example for all of us. For, at the end of the story, the monk is described as one who has become released from the wheel of rebirth during his lifetime.[46]

The monk is a Buddhist monk; he lives in a Buddhist monastery in a northern country called Jina, perhaps China. He is thus probably a Tibetan monk or some other sort of Mahayana monk—which is to say, a shaman and a magician. The power that he has is one that is shared by Hindu yogis as well: 'By their own powers over time and space, yogis and female yogis here can stand somewhere else, wherever they wish.'[47] The text lists other people from the annals of Hindu mythology who have had similar powers:

> While Vishnu remained asleep in the ocean of milk, he was born as a man on earth (Krishna); while Indra remains on his throne in heaven, he goes down to earth to receive the sacrifice; though Krishna was only one person, he became a thousand for the many kings who are his devotees, and for the thousands of women who were his mistresses, by indulging in the game (*lila*) of partial incarnation. In this same way, through the power of the understanding of Rudra, Jivata and the Brahmin and all the others who had been imagined by the monk went to whatever city they had imagined.[48]

Even ordinary people become what they concentrate on, *volens nolens*; this is the power that drives the machine of rebirth. Extraordinary people, however, can do this on purpose, and without dying. Vishnu, Indra, Krishna, and Rudra are gods. The imaginings of gods are a thousandfold more powerful than the imaginings of yogis and monks. And Rudra (in this text, at least) is both the supreme God and the supreme yogi.

Rudra is the warp upon which we all weave our dreams; he is the fluid in which we all flow together like particles in suspension. He is the place where we all meet in our dreams, the infinity where our parallel lives converge. The text tells us that the lives the monk imagined could not see one another, living as they did in separate universes, except through the knowledge of Rudra.[49] This last phrase is, I think, purposely ambiguous: it means that only people who know Rudra—in particular, who know that they are Rudra—can meet the people of their dreams (or meet the people that they were in their former lives and will be in their future lives). But it also means that only through the fact that *Rudra knows them* can they hope to bridge the gap between the apparently separate souls; that Rudra will show them that they are one another, because they are he. For though, as Rama points out, Rudra is merely a character in someone's dream—the monk's dream, at first, and the swan's dream, at last[50]—he is also the dreamer of all dreams, including the dream of the one who dreams him, the dream of the monk. Thus, when the text says that Jivata lives in a universe in a corner of the mind,[51] the immediate meaning is that it is a corner of the mind of the monk. But as the tale unfolds we come to understand that the monk himself exists only in the corner of another mind, Rudra's mind. Moreover, where the monk merely dreams of Rudra, the latter produces the monk in a more direct fashion: the monk is a partial incarnation of Rudra, an atom flowing in his veins. Rudra is 'made of Jivata and the others', the text says.

Thus our story takes place on three levels of thought that are also three levels of existence. We begin on the most obvious level, with our assumption that dreams are basically different from reality. On this level, animals actually change from one form to another when they die. Mind and matter are distinct; though they may interact and influence one another, they are made of different stuff. On the middle level, we encounter the possibility of transforming mind into matter and matter into mind. Here is the level where people dream, or think, about assuming another form, and so assume it. This middle level has two subdivisions: truly enlightened people, who understand that mind and matter are not essentially different things and may intentionally use their minds to bring about a change in the forms of matter—or rather, an apparent change; while those who are not truly enlightened are forced to undergo what they think to be real changes of form, though these changes too are merely apparent. Finally, on the highest level, we find the undifferentiated substance that always is both mind and matter, that underlies both the apparent changes of material form and the less obvious transmutations that mental forces exert upon apparent matter. On this level, we realize that nothing ever changes into anything else, that everything was there all along, and that everything was, for want of a better word, God, all along.

Despite Rudra's extraordinary ontological status, his actual mental processes are flawed like those of even the best of his dream creatures—the monk. The monk, who unknowingly imitates Rudra's 'play' (*lila*), begins dispassionately enough, but as soon as he imagines a person with passions (the earthy Jivata), he is caught up in those passions himself, forced to follow the game into realms he had not intended to explore. So, too, Rudra is caught up in his own sport; he is 'amazed' to see what creatures people the brave new world of his imagination. He too has karmic residues—more than anyone else, since he experiences *everyone's* lives.[52] Though he is the mould that cuts the forms, those forms also create themselves, beyond his control, once the process is set in motion. Like the monk, Rudra discovers that creation inevitably leads to imperfection, to the self-perpetuating desire to go on creating. Like the monk, Rudra indulges his frivolity, his creative urge. Even Rudra, then, is not a true model of freedom from karma; not even Rudra can remain deaf to the songs of the sirens he imagines.

For 'pure' play does not remain pure for long. When Rudra acts 'for the sake of play/sport/amusement/fun', or 'for the sheer hell of it' (*lilartham*), we might also translate the term, 'art for art's sake'. This same 'art' is implicit in the word usually translated as 'illusion', *maya*, which may be related to the Sanskrit verb 'to make' (*ma*). *Maya* is what Rudra 'makes' (or 'finds') when he imagines the universe; *maya* is his art. To say that the universe is an illusion is not to say that it is unreal; it is to say that it is not what it seems to be, that it is something constantly being *made.* Similar concepts cluster together in English around the derivatives of the Latin word for play (*ludo*, as in delusion, illusion, and so forth) and around the word 'play' itself (play as drama, as swordplay, as the play of light that causes mirages, as the ambiguity and double image implicit in wordplay).[53] These word clusters delineate a universe full of beauty and motion that enchants us all. Yet *maya* is often associated with evil in Indian texts, for it is the trick of the mind that causes us to become, literally, deadly serious about what begins in a spirit of play. *Maya* is what makes us dream, and die.

Caillois concludes his essay with a

speculation about the playfulness of the dream of God, from a Western point of view:

> The most rugged of theologians, in every period and of every persuasion, those who have dared to venture to the brink of the dizzy precipice of metaphysics, those who are mathematically cool and precise, have all agreed in assuming (one might say unanimously) that the relation between God and the world is like that which an all-powerful Spirit—a spirit that has no need to use its power, that scorns to impose its will, absentminded, impish, overgenerous—has with its Dream (solely through an excess of excellence), without even being aware of it. The Dream is the unfathomable, the inscrutable Universe that He lets emanate from Himself, a heedless and needless fantasy, perhaps.[54]

India provides a challenge to the 'unanimity' of this theological view, for it sees the dream of Rudra as one that he becomes aware of, and one that is not 'needless' once it has begun, though it might have been needless at the very beginning of the game.

If Rudra is thus caught in his own coils, is

there no one who is impervious, safe, out of bounds? There seems to be one: Vasishtha. Like the monk and Rudra, he is able to make his dreams come true, and not merely his dreams, but even his conscious didactic examples. Moreover, Vasishtha is not 'amazed' at the things that happen in his story, not even at the fact that his story turns out to be true. He creates not out of idle curiosity or even a spirit of playfulness, but to teach Rama a lesson. Unlike the Brahmin in the monk's dream, who, although a Brahmin, was not a particularly subtle theologian or accomplished sage, Vasishtha knows all the answers; he alone never seems to be fooled.

Vasishtha is the key to the paradox of the dreamer dreamt. The tale of the monk involved us in what Douglas Hofstadter has called a Strange Loop or a Tangled Hierarchy.[55] Each dream seems to be nested inside another, until, when we encounter the final, innermost dream, it is identified with the outermost dream: Rudra is the monk who is dreaming about Rudra. What we thought was a spiral turns out to be a kind of Möbius strip, which bends in on itself forever. This bothers Rama: 'How could a hundred Rudras be made by Rudra who was himself made in someone's dream?' Tangled hierarchies of this sort abound in logic, as a special kind of paradox of which perhaps the most famous is the self-referential paradox of Epimenides, the Cretan who stated, 'All Cretans are liars.' Lewis Carroll, who was fascinated by paradoxes of this sort, dramatized the same one that animated the tale of the monk's dream: Alice dreams that the Red King dreams of her. In visual form, such tangled hierarchies appear in the etchings of Escher, such as 'Drawing Hands': a hand draws a picture of a hand that draws the first hand.[56] In literature and art, these paradoxes can be 'solved', if one cheats by stepping back out of the frame altogether, to what Hofstadter calls the 'inviolate level'. The answer to Lewis Carroll's question, 'Who dreamed the dream?' is, 'Lewis Carroll,' and it is Escher who drew the hands. In our Hindu myth, we are tempted to step back in rhythm with all the other characters who leap from frame to frame: we move from Rudra who is dreamt by the swan go into his dream and wake up the people who are dreaming him, we cannot rest confident in our assumption that *our* level of the story is the final 'inviolate' level. If there *is* one inviolate level, it is the level of the Godhead, the impersonal continuum beyond even Rudra. This is the level of the universal soul, the source of all mental images that assume material form. For though monks and great sages and poets and gods can project themselves into physical bodies whenever they want to, all of us—princes and harlots and bees and professors and readers—helplessly spin, out of our desires, the lives that we have inherited from our former selves. Sooner or later, our dreams do become real, whether we want them to or not, whether they are nightmares or wishes that we long to have fulfilled. The difference between most of us and Indian sages like Vasishtha is that we are unaware of our dreams, unaware of our repeated lives, or rather, unwilling to accept the disquieting, but challenging, possibility that the former lives and dreams may be as real, or unreal, as our waking experiences and thoughts.

KARMIC MEMORY TRACES

In many Indian texts that begin on an apparently more realistic nature, though they often go on to plunge deep into the doctrine of illusion, the mythology of reincarnation jumps the barrier of rebirth, imagining the survival of consciousness on the other side. Such stories suggest that each of us, in our present lives, may at any moment be awakened to the memory of another, lost life. That we all constantly reinvent ourselves out of the scraps of the past, so that, in a sense, we are always imitating our past selves. The signals we send to ourselves from our former lives are wake-up calls, like the message the Chippendale Mupp, one of the creatures in Dr. Seuss's *Sleep Book*, sends to himself: at bedtime, he bites the end tuft on his *very* long tail, so that the ouch will work its way up the whole tail and, finally, wake him up in the morning.

The myths of karma ask: Where is memory, in the mind or in the body? How can our bodies remember things that our minds have forgotten? And here we must return to take a closer look at those karmic memory traces that we encountered in the story of the monk's dream. Hinduism assumes that when the body dies, the soul transmigrates, taking with it the dead person's karma, the moral record of good and bad actions committed in all former lives. Indian philosophy locates memory in the *manas*, a combination of mind and heart: like the heart, it is a physical organ in the body, and like the mind, it is where you learn calculus, and like both mind and heart, it is where you fall in love—thus doubly blurring the Cartesian distinction between mind and body. However, although the transmigrating soul in Hinduism usually loses its memory as it crosses the boundary of rebirth and sheds its body, some particularly gifted and/or lucky people can remember their previous births. Some branches of Indian philosophy, therefore, locate memory along with karma in (or more precisely on) the soul, without, however, totally divorcing it from the body.

The karma theory tells us that we have lived lives that we cannot remember and hence cannot feel. We can remember some things in life in our minds, and perhaps, therefore, in our souls, but other things can only be remembered with our bodies, which do not survive the trip across the barrier of death. According to the karma theory, however, memory is not all there is; there is also a reality of unrecalled experience that gives a kind of validity to our connection with lives that we do not recall. The karma theory recognizes the parallelism between events forgotten within a single life—the events of early childhood, or the things that we repress or that (in Hindu mythology) we forget as the result of a curse—and the events forgotten from a previous life.[58] It also recognizes a similarity in the ways in which we sometimes half-recall these various sorts of events, often with a sense of *déjà vu*, the feeling that one sometimes has, on seeing someone or someplace for the first time, that one has seen it before. We remember something that we cannot remember, from a lost past, through the power of the invisible tracks or traces left behind on our souls by those events; these traces are the *vasanas*, 'perfumes', scents that are the impressions of anything remaining unconsciously in the mind, the present consciousness of past perceptions, the *impressions* of anything remaining unconsciously in the mind, the present *consciousness* of past perceptions.[59] These *vasanas* are what a king in a Sanskrit play (a man who has been cursed to forget his wife[60]) has in mind when he says:

> Even a happy man may be overcome by passionate longing when he sees beautiful things or hears sweet sounds. Perhaps he is remembering something he was not conscious of before that moment, the loves of a former life, firmly rooted in the impressions of lingering emotions.[61]

The bits of experience that Hindus call the 'karmic memory traces' cling to our transmigrating souls even in new bodies, loose threads trailing not merely from a former life within this lifespan but from a previous life, a previous incarnation. One commentator remarks that it is impossible to shake off these impressions even after thousands of lives.[62]

Such 'perfumes' also correspond in many ways to the social chemosignals that Martha McClintock has studied, olfactory clues to social behaviour that are handed down genetically (which is, in a sense, through rebirths), generally unconscious clues that influence our emotions. Parents, conveyors of the more general genetic inheritance stretching back over generations, are the carriers of 'social chemosignals' that are handed down in the DNA and are responsible for what McClintock termed, 'the effect of a previous life on one's current life',[63] a power that Marcel Proust famously attributed to the taste/flavour/perfume of little tea-soaked madeleines from Combray. Appropriately, McClintock named one group of these chemosignals, closely related to what she has called pheromones, after the *vasanas* of Hindu philosophy:

> [S]ocial chemosignals are remarkably similar to the medieval Sanskrit term *vasanas*. *Vasana*, the singular noun, is derived from the Sanskrit term *vas*, meaning 'to perfume'... The term is used to explain why a person has a tendency to react to a situation in a

> particular way. We find it useful to adopt this philosophical term in our classification of human social chemosignals because both its etymology and its functional definition are so close to the findings from our empirical psychological data...Vasanas are those unconscious chemosignals whose functional effects are related to or predicted by their odour qualities when they are experienced consciously...The power of subconscious odours to evoke emotional memory-derived experience in humans is widely recognized...Because they are not necessarily conscious, the term *vasana* may be more appropriate than 'unconscious odours,' which is an oxymoron.[64]

The Cycle of Memory and Forgetting

The unconscious memories of past lives, the *vasanas*, predispose the transmigrating soul to act in one way or another in its new life. It retains some sort of magnetic attachment to its old body and, with it, to its old personality. Even if we cannot remember who we were, we are reborn in the shadow of our previous personality. The soul gets typecast.

This belief is also expressed in Hindu texts that imagine the reincarnating soul meditating on its next life in the womb of the soul's future mother, where it (not yet he or she) not only remains fully conscious but remembers its previous lives in agonizing detail:

> Then it begins to remember its many previous existences in the wheel of rebirth, and that depresses it, and it tosses from side to side, thinking, 'I won't ever do *that* again, as soon as I get out of this womb. I will do everything I can, so that I won't become an embryo again.' It thinks in this way as it remembers the hundreds of miseries of birth that it experienced before, in the power of fate. Then, as time goes by, the embryo turns around, head down, and in the ninth or tenth month it is born. As it comes out, it is hurt by the wind of procreation; it comes out crying, because it is pained by the misery in its heart. When it has come out of the womb, it falls into an unbearable swoon, but it regains consciousness when the air touches it. Then Vishnu's deluding power of illusion assails him, and when his soul has been deluded by it, he loses his knowledge. As soon as the living creature has lost his

> knowledge, he becomes a baby. After that he becomes a young boy, then an adolescent, and then an old man. And then he dies and is born again as a human. Thus, he wanders on the wheel of rebirth like the bucket on the wheel of a well.[65]

Chagrin at the memory of previous mistakes and despair at the realization that one will make them all again in this life, too, is what makes the baby cry as he enters the world. The *Laws of Manu* (c. 375 CE), the classical Sanskrit text of Hindu law, promises many upwardly mobile transmigrations, but not for everyone: 'Through the repetition of their evil actions, men of little intelligence experience miseries in womb after womb in this world.'[66]

Reincarnation is generally regarded as a fresh start, but the tabula is not always quite so rasa as more simplistic treatments of the doctrine assume. The goal of liberation theology, Hindu style, is to untangle the knots of karma, to achieve *moksha*, freedom from the same old same old in life after life. For a Hindu, this means to break out altogether from *samsara* (the cycle of transmigration), but it could also mean to be free to go forward without the compulsion for self-imitation. For people find it difficult to kick the Lethe habit. In many ways the *vasanas* that return to the reborn soul correspond not just to the unconscious as we have come to understand it but more particularly to the repressed unconscious that *returns*, in Freud's formulation.[67] Freud also referred to a 'memory trace' (*Erinnerungsspur*) that was not yet a part of conscious memory.[68]

As we saw in the tale of the monk's dream, the swan, or wild goose, a natural and cross-cultural symbol of periodic return, is the emblem of both the individual soul and the mind of god, in this case Rudra. In this metaphysical world, we remember both our dreams and our rebirths—much the same thing—when we awaken from our primary amnesia, which makes us forget that we are god. That story, as we have seen, goes on to raise other metaphysical issues, but these passages make several important points for the topic at hand. The transition to a new life can take place either by thinking of something or by suffering a violent death, for dreaming and dying are conflated. Both dreaming and dying are brought on by over-indulgence in the pleasures of the senses, and those same pleasures of the senses determine the content of the dream or the new life. Indeed, sensual appeal is what attracts the soul to the next life: love, admiration (even, sometimes, in its negative aspect of jealousy), obsession, fascination. Rudra himself (the supreme deity, who is regarded here, as often in Hindu mythology, as existing on a level that encompasses the tasks and powers of the Creator) is caught up in this round of attraction, but he is also the source of our own attractions, the source to which we return when the cycle has played itself out.

And so in each new life, we pretend, once again, to be who we are, repeating lines from an earlier script even when we think that we are improvising or that we are not performing at all. We cannot escape from our own previous character, our desire, which sticks like tar to the transmigrating soul. Our memory of those ancient desires is partly accidental, partly not so accidental. Hinduism offers several different praxes designed to help us remember our former lives, just as psychoanalysis claims to help us remember our dreams. For most of us, however, such memories remain largely unconscious and inaccessible.

THE GOD WHO FORGOT HE WAS GOD

All of us tend to forget that we are god, according to the doctrine of Hindu idealism in the *Yogavasishtha*. But divinity is a continuum; some creatures are more divine than others, and some gods are more divine in certain texts than in others. The philosophical and mythological assertion that all humans are (conscious or unconscious) incarnations of a deity is enacted in the many rituals in which the worshipper masquerades as the god (through the use of masks, for instance). The *Yogavasishtha* depicts humans who forget that the god Shiva, as Rudra, is the very substance of consciousness, but in other texts, Shiva himself forgets who he is and engages in unconscious self-imitation when his wife Parvati tricks him by masquerading as another woman.[69] The chain continues when Shiva and Parvati become incarnate not merely in all human beings but in particular human beings (called partial incarnations) who slip in and out of consciousness of their incarnational status.

A Sanskrit text composed in Assam in the tenth or eleventh century explores the human complications that can arise out of such a partial (re)incarnation.[70] In this text, Shiva and Parvati impersonate a human king and queen on three increasingly specific levels: First is the general philosophical doctrine that all creatures are made of *brahman*, and hence the king and queen are part of the godhead embodied in Shiva and Parvati. Second is the implicit metaphysical incarnation based on the belief that all men and women are forms of Shiva and Parvati, rather than of other deities, for human beings are all marked with the signs of the god Shiva and his consort, the male and female sexual organs, *lingam* and *yoni*.[71] And third, the proximate cause, is the explicit impersonation of the king by Shiva, necessitated by a sage's curse,[72] a common cause of the incarnation of Hindu gods as humans.

The incarnations (or avatars) of the god

Vishnu, particularly Rama and Krishna, have a more particular awareness of their own divinity, yet even they often forget their divine natures. In the *Mahabharata*, Krishna often forgets he is god until someone else—a mortal or, occasionally, another god—or, occasionally, Krishna himself remembers. In later texts such as the tenth-century *Bhagavata Purana*, however, Krishna never forgets. Indeed, when Krishna is still a little child, he sometimes remembers not only that he is god but that he was previously incarnate as Rama, recalling, when he is drifting between sleeping and waking, his earlier birth as Rama.[73] He is also firmly in control of his knowledge of his own divinity when he deals with other people (including his mother) whom he allows to forget who he is because they cannot sustain the intensity of their brief visions of his true nature.[74]

Rama, too, often forgets his divinity. When Rama publicly doubts that his wife Sita was unfaithful to him, the gods ask how he can do this, adding, 'Can you not know that you are the best of all the gods?' Rama, uncomprehending, says, 'I think of myself as a man, as Rama, the son of king Dasharatha. Tell me who I really am, and who my father is, and where I come from.'[75] Sheldon Pollock has argued convincingly that in order to achieve his purpose of killing the demon Ravana, Rama must become truly human, for Ravana has secured a boon that no one but a human being can kill him. And to be truly human is to forget that you are god, which Rama must do—at least until after Ravana's death. Moreover, taking on a human body is the consequence of wrong knowledge,[76] for true knowledge would have brought enlightenment and freedom from the wheel of rebirth. The very act of incarnation would destroy the incarnation's true knowledge of his divinity, but, in addition (as we have seen), in the process of being born, the newborn child must lose his knowledge. Therefore, an embodied avatar cannot possibly remember who he has been; the very fact of human birth robs him of the capacity to remember his past existences. Other commentators argued that Rama had intentionally become ignorant or that he merely pretended to forget who he was.[77] In other retellings of the narrative, too, Rama insists that he merely pretended to subject Sita to an ordeal and, presumably, pretended to forget that he was god.[78] If the gods themselves are subject to this constant forgetfulness of their true nature and equally constant reawakening to it, how could we mere mortals hope to do any better?

When the incarnate god does remember that he is God, he sometimes reminds forgetful mortals of his true nature but often, out of compassion, allows them to forget it.

In a famous passage of the *Bhagavad Gita*, Arjuna looks inside the mouth of his friend Krishna, who is Vishnu, and sees him devouring the universe in his aspect of the Lord of Doomsday. But then he spreads his *maya* over the stunned and terrified Arjuna so that Arjuna can once again just regard Krishna as his pal.

The *Bhagavata Purana*, composed in Sanskrit in South India, probably during the tenth century of the Common Era, adds another layer to the image when it tells a story about the same incarnate god Krishna when he was a little boy, here with his mortal foster-mother, Yashodha:

> One day when the children were playing, they reported to Yashodha, 'Krishna has eaten dirt.' Yashodha took Krishna by the hand and scolded him and said, 'You naughty boy, why have you eaten dirt? These boys, your friends, and your elder brother say so.'
>
> 'Mother, I have not,' said Krishna. 'They are all lying. If you believe them instead of me, look at my mouth yourself.'
>
> 'Then open up,' she said to the god, who had in play taken the form of a human child; and he opened his mouth.
>
> Then she saw in his mouth the whole universe, with the far corners of the sky, and the wind, and lightning, and the orb of the Earth with its mountains and oceans, and the moon and stars, and space itself; and she saw her own village and herself. She became frightened and confused, thinking, 'Is this a dream or an illusion fabricated by God? Or is it a delusion in my own mind? For God's power of delusion inspires in me such false beliefs as, "I exist", "This is my

> husband", "This is my son".' When she had come to understand true reality in this way, God spread his magic illusion in the form of maternal love. Instantly Yashodha lost her memory of what had occurred. She took her son on her lap and was as she had been before, but her heart was flooded with even greater love for God, whom she regarded as her son.[79]

What could be more personal, more 'deeply rooted in the things of this world', more literally *down to earth* or *earthy* than a small boy lying about eating *dirt*? But taking off from this modest moment the myth plummets down and turns the universe inside out, shifting gears entirely, into the warp-speed of *mythos*. Yashodha, like Arjuna, cannot sustain the vertiginous vision of the universe beyond the world that she has always regarded as real. T. S. Eliot pointed out (in *Burnt Norton*), 'Humankind cannot bear very much reality'; apparently, humankind can't bear very much *un*reality, either, or very much of what the text presents as an alternative reality.

In the *Mahabharata*, the sage Markandeya,

Vishnu shows his cosmic form 'Vishvarupa' to Arjuna and Yashodha (A version from Punjab Hills, Bilaspur, c. 1740).
Source: Wikimedia Commons

Vishnu asleep in the cosmic ocean, reclining on Ananta (Attributed to Durga Master, c. 1780-90, Mehrangarh Museum Trust).
Source: Wikimedia Commons

one of the few who have survived the cosmic doomsday, stumbles into the mouth of Vishnu who is asleep in the cosmic ocean; there he sees the entire universe, until Vishnu allows him to come out again.[80] The *Matsya Purana*, composed in the early centuries of the present era, retells the story and adds new questions:

> After Vishnu had burnt the universe to ashes at doomsday and then flooded it with water, he slept in the midst of the cosmic ocean. The sage Markandeya was swallowed by the god and he roamed inside his belly for many thousands of years, visiting the sacred places on earth. One day he slipped out of the god's mouth and saw the world and the ocean shrouded in complete darkness. He did not recognize himself there, because of God's illusion, and he became terrified. Then he saw the sleeping god [Vishnu], and he was amazed, wondering, 'Am I crazy, or dreaming? I must be imagining that the world has disappeared, for such a calamity could never really happen.' Then he was swallowed again, and, as soon as he was back in the belly of the god, he thought his vision had been a dream.

So, as before, he roamed the earth for hundreds of years, and then again he slipped out of Vishnu's mouth. This time he saw, in the middle of the cosmic ocean, a little boy hidden in the branches of a banyan tree, a boy who blazed so like the sun that Markandeya could not bear to look at him. 'I think I have seen this once before,' mused the sage. 'I think I'm being fooled by the illusion of God.' In confusion and terror, Markandeya began to swim away, but Vishnu said, 'Do not be afraid, my son. Come here. I am your father.' Markandeya bowed to him with love, and Vishnu taught him His true nature and commanded him to return inside His belly. Then Vishnu swallowed Markandeya once more, and the sage lived there in peace.[81]

Markandeya at first thinks that some sort of illusion is being foisted upon him, but he gets it backwards: when he falls out of Vishnu's mouth, he feels that he has entered an illusion, not knowing that he has just *escaped* from the illusion. And when he has an intimation of *déjà vu*—which in his case is a true realization because he has, in fact, already experienced the vision once before—he is all the more convinced that he is at that moment experiencing an illusion. Eventually, he understands the truth of the vision and is released from his delusions; he realizes that he and Vishnu are one and the same, the soul and God, each containing the other.

When the story is retold yet again in the *Kurma Purana*, even the gods are victims of illusion:

> When the world was in darkness, Vishnu slept in the middle of the cosmic ocean. A lotus grew out of his navel. Brahma came to him and said, 'Tell me, who are you?' Vishnu replied, 'I am Vishnu, creator of the universe. All the worlds, and you yourself, are inside me. And who are you?' Brahma replied, '*I* am the creator, self-created, and everything is inside *me*.' Vishnu then entered Brahma's body and saw all three worlds in his belly. Astonished, he came out of Brahma's mouth and said, 'Now you must enter my belly in the same way and see the worlds.' And so Brahma entered Vishnu's belly and saw all the worlds. Then, since Vishnu had shut all the openings, Brahma came out of Vishnu's navel and rested on the lotus.[82]

Again we encounter the logical dilemma of two minds, each creating and enclosing the other.

When Arjuna and Yashodha encounter the mouth of God, they emerge momentarily from the illusion (*maya*) that until now they have existed outside of God; it is as if they awaken from a dream. The several versions of the story of Markandeya add the insight that God, too, is a dreamer, dreaming us even as we (and, perhaps, other gods) are dreaming *Him*.

We may ask: Does the dream ever end? The texts suggest that doomsday is nothing but one dream ending, so that another can begin.

NOTES

1 This extended essay is based upon two much earlier essays of mine, the first written when I was still publishing under the name of Wendy Doniger O'Flaherty and was working on what eventually became a book, *Dreams, Illusion, and Other Realities* (Chicago: University of Chicago Press, 1984). I tried out my ideas about dreams first in 'Illusion and Reality in the *Yogavasishtha,* or, The Scientific Proof of Mythical Experience,' in the Spring 1981 issue of *Quadrant*; then in the 1982 Foerster Lecture on the Immortality of the Soul, in Berkeley, on March 8, 1982, and then as one of the Mead-Swing Lectures at Oberlin College, on March 25, 1982. I then published 'The Dream Narrative and the Indian Doctrine of Illusion' in *Daedalus* (Summer 1982, pp. 93-113), and lectured on 'The paradox of the dreamer dreamt: the Red

King and the Hindu God' at the annual meeting of the Lewis Carroll Society of North America, The Newberry Library, Chicago, April 1985. I turned to other aspects of dreams in 'Other Peoples' Religions, Other Peoples' *Kama* and *Karma*' in *The Stranger's Religion: Fascination and Fear* (ed. Anna Lanstrom. Notre Dame, Indiana: Notre Dame University Press, 2004, pp. 79-98), and to the related theme of dreams and memories and incarnation, in 'Wake Up Calls: Some Ancient Hindu Myths' in *Parabola* in 2005 (reprinted, somewhat revised, in *The Inner Journey: Views from the Hindu Tradition*, [ed. Margaret H. Case. Sandpoint, Idaho: Morning Light Press, 2007], pp. 212-221) and 'Forgetting and Re-awakening to Incarnation', in *On Hinduism* (New York: Oxford University Press, 2014, pp. 107-115). The present essay includes some material that was eventually incorporated into those books and articles, as well as some that was not.

2 Plato, *Theaetetus* 157E-158E.

3 In addition to the overall dream structure of the two Alice books, Lewis Carroll describes the encounter between Alice and the Red King who is, she is told, dreaming of her. As Martin Gardner remarks on this passage, 'The Berkeleyan theme troubled Carroll as it troubles all Platonists'. In *The Annotated Alice* (New York: Penguin Books, 1970), p. 238.

4 Roger Caillois, 'Logical and Philosophical Problems of the Dream', in *The Dream and Human Societies,* edited by G. E. von Grunebaum and Roger Caillois (Berkeley: University of California Press, 1966), pp. 33-35. The stories of the dream adventure appear in *The Dream Adventure,* edited by Roger Caillois (New York: The Orion Press, 1963).

5 See, for example, 'The Circular Ruins', in *Labyrinths* (New York: Penguin, 1970), pp. 72-77.

6 My favourite example of this genre in the fiction of Eliade is 'Nights at Serampore', in *Two Tales of the Occult* (New York: Herder and Herder, 1970), pp. 72-77.

7 Caillois, 'Logical and Philosophical Problems', p. 46.

8 The text I have used is the *Yogavasishthamaharamayana* of Valmiki, with the commentary *Vasishthamaharamayanatat paryaprakasha*, 2 volumes, edited by W. L. S. Pansikar (Bombay: Nirnaya Sagara Press, 1918).

9 Cf. C. R. Sarma, *The Ramayana in Telugu and Tamil* (Madras: Lawrence Verry Incorporated, 1973). A variant of one of the tales from the *Yogavasishtha* was recorded by John Hinton Knowles in Kashmir in 1893; another variant of the same tale was told to me in August 1980, in Mysore, by Mrs. Lalita Handoo, who heard it from her great-aunt in Kashmir.

10 *Yogavasishtha* 6.1.62.1-31, 6.1.63.1-75, 6.1.64.1-8.

11 Stith Thompson, *Motif Index of Folk Literature*, revised edition, 6 volumes, (Bloomington, Indiana: Indiana University Press, 1955-58), motif D 2041.5, volume 2, p. 308.

12 *Yogavasishtha* 6.1.64.6-13, 6.1.65.6-8, 6.1.69.1-6.

13 For the construction of lives as *bricolage*, see my essay 'Inside and Outside the Mouth of God: The Boundary between Myth and Reality', which appeared in the Spring 1980 issue of *Daedalus*, pp. 93-125.

14 For the argument that common sense is a cultural construct that differs in different times and places, see 'Common Sense as a Cultural System' by Clifford Geertz, which appeared in *Antioch Review*, vol. 33, 1975, pp. 5-26.

15 Commentary on *Yogavasishtha* 6.1.69.4.

16 *Yogavasishtha* 6.1.63.6.

17 I am indebted to David Shulman for the formulation of this paragraph, and to A. K. Ramanujan for the suggestion that everyone makes the distinction between the real and the unreal, somewhere along a shifting continuum.

18 *Yogavasishtha* 6.1.65.10-20; 6.1.66.1-28; 6.1.67.1-6.

19 *Yogavasishtha* 6.1.66.6.

20 Commentary on *Yogavasishtha* 6.1.65.13.

21 *Yogavasishtha* 6.1.69.2.

22 Commentary on *Yogavasishtha* 6.1.67.4.

23 *Yogavasishtha* 6.1.63.21.
24 *Kumarasambhava* of Kalidasa (Bombay: Nirnaya Sagara Press, 1955), 1.30.
25 *Bhagavata Purana* with the commentary of Shridhara (Bombay: Venkateshvara Steam Press, 1832; rept. Motilal Banarsidass, Delhi, 1983), 4.2 8.51-64.
26 *Yogavasishtha* 6.1.63.1-3.
27 *Yogavasishtha* 6.1.62.7.
28 *Yogavasishtha* 6.1.63.19; 6.1.62.20-21.
29 *Yogavasishtha* 6.1.62.22-6.
30 *Yogavasishtha* 6.1.66.22-4.
31 Introduction to *Yogavasishtha* 6.1.62.1.
32 *Yogavasishtha* 6.1.62.32.
33 *Yogavasishtha* 6.1.63.17.
34 *Yogavasishtha* 6.1.65.3-7.
35 *Yogavasishtha* 6.1.63.9, 6.1.62.7.
36 *Yogavasishtha* 6.1.62.5.
37 *Yogavasishtha* 6.1.63.10-11.
38 *Yogavasishtha* 6.1.63.36.
39 Commentary on *Yogavasishtha* 6.1.62.6.
40 *Yogavasishtha* 6.1. 63.13.
41 On *Yogavasishtha* 6.1.62.1.
42 *Yogavasishtha* 6.1.62.6.
43 *Yogavasishtha* 6.1.63.10.
44 *Yogavasishtha* 6.1.65.12.
45 Commentary on *Yogavasishtha* 6.1.67.1.
46 *Yogavasishtha* 6.1.67.6.
47 *Yogavasishtha* 6.1.64.28.

48 *Yogavasishtha* 6.1.66.29-34.
49 *Yogavasishtha* 6.1.64.21
50 *Yogavasishtha* 6.1.69.4.
51 *Yogavasishtha* 6.1.63.41.
52 For the karma of the gods, see Wendy Doniger O'Flaherty, *Karma and Rebirth in Classical Indian Traditions* (Berkeley: University of California Press, 1980), pp. 23-27.
53 Johan Huizinga's *Homo Ludens: A Study of the Play Element in Culture* (Boston: Beacon Press, 1938/1955) is the definitive discussion of this theme.
54 Caillois, 'Logical and Philosophical Problems', p. 52.
55 Douglas R. Hofstadter, *Gotdel, Escber, Bach: An Eternal Golden Braid* (New York: Basic Books, 1979; and Vintage Books, 1980), pp. 686-92.
56 See ibid., p. 690, for Hofstadter's analysis of this drawing.
57 I am indebted to Alan Dundes for this distinction between cumulative and nesting tales.
58 Robert P. Goldman, 'Karma, Guilt, and Buried Memories: Public Fantasy and Private Reality in Traditional India'. *Journal of the American Oriental Society*, vol. 105, no. 3 (1985).
59 Sir Monier Monier-Williams, *Sanskrit-English Dictionary*, p. 947, s.v. *vasana*.
60 Wendy Doniger, 'The Clever Wife in Indian Mythology'. In *Incompatible Visions: South Asian*

Religions in History and Culture. Essays in Honor of David M. Knipe (ed. James Blumenthal. Madison: University of Madison-Wisconsin, Center for South Asia, 2005), pp. 185-203.

61 Kalidasa, *Abhijnanashakuntalam* (with the commentary of Raghava. Bombay: Nirnaya Sagara Press, 1958), 5.2.

62 *Raghavabhatta* 9, cited by Goldman, 'Karma'.

63 Martha McClintock and Suma Jacob, Bethanne Zelano, and Davinder J. S. Hayreh. 'Pheromones and Vasanas: The Functions of Social Chemosignals'. In *Evolutionary Psychology and Motivation*, Volume 48 of the Nebraska Symposium on Motivation, ed. Jeffrey A. French, et al. (Lincoln, Nebraska: University of Nebraska Press, 2001), pp. 75-112.

64 Ibid., p. 99.

65 *Markandeya Purana* (with commentary. Bombay: Venkateshvara Steam Press, 1890), 10.1-7, 11.1-21.

66 Manu, *The Laws of Manu* (trans. Wendy Doniger with Brian K. Smith. Harmondsworth: Penguin Books, 1991), 12.74.

67 Sigmund Freud, *Moses and Monotheism* (trans. Katherine Jones. New York: Vintage Books, 1939), p. 162.

68 Freud, 'The Unconscious'. In *Collected Papers*, 4 (1925), pp. 98-136.

69 Doniger, *The Bedtrick: Tales of Sex and Masquerade*

(Chicago: University of Chicago Press, 2000), pp. 17-20.

70 *Kalika Purana* (ed. Sri Biswanarayan Sastri. Varanasi: Chowkhamba Sanskrit Series Office, 1972), 49-52; Wendy Doniger O'Flaherty, *Siva: The Erotic Ascetic*, [*Asceticism and Eroticism in the Mythology of Siva*], New York: Galaxy, 1981), pp. 206-7.

71 *Mahabharata* (ed. V. S. Sukthankar et al. Poona: Bhandarkar Oriental Research Institute, 1933-69.) 13, app. 1, no. 5, p. 69; Doniger, *The Bedtrick*, p. 397.

72 This text takes basic themes from the story of Rama: Shiva is cursed to become human as Vishnu is cursed to take on a human incarnation in the *Ramayana*, and Chandrashekhara is born as Rama is born, out of portions of a god (there Vishnu, here Shiva) distributed to a group of queens. But instead of producing multiple children (as Rama's brothers are produced), the portions here come together to make a single composite child.

73 Goldman, 'Karma', p. 420.

74 Doniger O'Flaherty, *Dreams*, pp. 109-10.

75 *Ramayana* of Valmiki (Baroda: Oriental Institute, 1960-75), 6.105.8-10.

76 Sheldon Pollock, '"Atmanam Manusam Manye": *Dharmakutam* on the divinity of Rama'. *Journal of the Oriental Institute, Baroda*, vol. 33, nos. 3-4 (March-June, 1984), p. 233.

77 Ibid., pp. 234-5, 242.

78 Wendy Doniger, *Splitting the Difference: Gender and Myth in Ancient Greece and India* (Chicago: The University of Chicago Press, 1999), pp. 9-27.

79 *Bhagavata Purana* 10.8.21-45; see Wendy Doniger, *The Implied Spider: Politics and Theology in Myth* (New York: Columbia University Press, 2nd ed., 2011), pp. 17-18.

80 *Mahabharata* 3.186.75-120.

81 *Matsya Purana* (Poona: Anandashrama Sanskrit Series 54, 1909), pp. 167-68.

82 *Kurma Purana* (Varanasi: All-India Kashiraj Press, 1972) 1.9.

ALSO FROM SPEAKING TIGER

THE LAW OF DESIRE

Rulings On Sex And Sexuality In India

MADHAVI MENON

Can a woman choose whom to marry if her father disapproves of the match? Does sex remain sex when it becomes work? Can a man become a woman because he feels like one? Is it the law's task to ensure heterosexuality? Does reproduction need to be regulated?

The State attempts, with law as its instrument, to answer these questions for us, through legislation and, when contested, through court judgments. This brilliantly insightful and superbly argued book calls into serious question the wisdom—indeed, the intent—of our lawmakers and the judiciary. Though India's laws and courts claim to know what they mean when they declare an expression of desire immoral or criminal, obscene or unnatural, upon inquiry, they turn out to be building on very weak and often casteist and patriarchal assumptions. Thus we have the law struggling to 'rescue' 'fallen women', for sex work cannot be work, but a sign of immorality; a Supreme Court judge can exonerate the artist M.F. Husain on charges of obscenity, but also claim that 'obscenity lies in the eyes of the beholder', leaving us wondering how, then, the law can ever define what's obscene; and while a court may declare that the 'third gender' has fundamental rights, no one really knows what fundamental rights have to do with gender in the first place.

Teacher and queer theorist Madhavi Menon—author of *Infinite Variety*, a celebrated study of desire in India—shows us the 'conundrums and paradoxes' that result when the law is entangled with sex and sexuality—and why we 'need to play with, rather than stay with, the Law of Desire'.